Presentation:

Of all the artists of the 20th century, without a doubt Joan Miró is the one who has attracted children's attention the most. Some people try to explain this by saying that his paintings are so much like children's paintings. Children, however, as well as their parents and their teachers, know that this is not true.

The thing is that Miró believed in his own language, —a language we all recognize immediately, and this language is based on simplicity, like children's language. Joan Miró always avoided complicated forms; he delighted in simple, balanced compositions and pure colours.

In order to be able to express himself in such a personal style, Joan Miró had to struggle and to work hard. This never frightened him. On the contrary, it stimulated him and encouraged him to work even harder.

We were very pleased to hear that a book was being published —this one, written by Fina Duran and illustrated by Pilarín Bayès— explaining to the youngsters the story of how Joan Miró became who he was. The simplicity of the language and the appropriateness of the drawings will help our young readers to get to know our great artist better and to discover his great passion: his profession.

We want to ask those of you who have this little book in your hands to do something: read it! We're sure you'll love it.

Rosa Maria MALET

It was the year 1892, when Barcelona was a much smaller city than it is today and above all much quieter. The people strolled along Fernando Street all dressed up in their best suits, with that traditional Sunday pastery under their arm that they had just bought at some special pastery shop where everything tasted so good...

The men greeted the passers-by they knew very politely with a tip of their hat and the ladies with a smile, as they looked out of the corner of their eye at the shops where the most fashionable dresses in the city were sold.

Very near that street with the exclusive shops there lived a man with big moustaches whose name was Miguel Miró, along with his wife Dolors Ferrà —a lady with a sweet look in her eye.

Guess what! On the 20th of April, that couple had a beautiful little baby boy who they named Joan. That little boy was to become the great Joan Miró.

Already very early in life that little boy demonstrated two things to his parents: first, that when he wanted something he would *not* give in; and second, that whenever he got hold of a piece of paper and some coloured pencils he would spend hours and hours drawing pictures and, above all, combining colours.

One day, after the evening meal, Mr. Miró mentioned to his wife how happy it would make him to see his son Joan carry on the trade. (Mr. Miró was a jeweller.) Since the boy liked to draw so much, he would have him take drawing lessons at some arts and crafts school so that when he was older he would be able to help him design beautiful pieces of jewellery.

Not many weeks after that, Mrs. Miró took little Joan, who was only seven at the time, to drawing classes at a school near their house, kept by a big hefty man by the name of Mr. Civil.

Joan was growing up and his interest in anything and everything artistic was as strong as ever. One day, his father decided that if Joan was to be successful, he had to go to the School of Commerce, because there he would learn the basic things that would help him be a good business man.

If we have to say the truth, we don't think Joan liked that school very much, but since his father didn't object to him studying at Llotja at the same time —the school where everyone who wanted to be an artist went— he went along with the idea.

One day, when Joan was sixteen, his father, with a very serious air, called him aside and told him that he had found a job for him as a shop assistant at Dalmau Oliveras Household Cleaning-Products and that there he could put into practice what he learned at the School of Commerce.

You can about imagine the poor boy working in that shop! He had told his father over and over that he did not want to be a shop assistant, but that he wanted to be an artist. You can be sure that he had told him all the possible ways he knew how to, but Mr. Miró was a very stubborn man and there was no way to convince him.

Joan got sadder and sadder and he started to get thinner and thinner until one day, two years after he started working for Mr. Dalmau, he came down with an illness called typhus.

His parents were very worried and decided to send him to Montroig* to recover, but first they promised him that they would never stand in his way again or stop him from becoming an artist, so he must have been quite happy in spite of his illness.

That good news did him more good than all the medicines the doctors had prescribed, and so he left in a happy mood for that little town in the Province of Tarragona.

A few days after his arrival he was feeling better already and he could take walks and wander through the fields, talking to the farmers and enjoying so much light after being used to the darkness of the narrow streets of Barcelona. Above all, he could see things. He could see the fields of hazelnut trees as they disappeared into the distance. He could see the nice little vegetable gardens, the cows, the donkeys, and all the other animals grazing so peaceably in the meadows.

* A town in Baix Camp, Tarragona.

With great enthusiasm, he began to paint everything around him, and by doing what he liked to do, he got better and better and was soon able to return to Barcelona.

Before he was nineteen, he was back in Barcelona, but everything had changed so much that it hardly looked like the same place.

He started going to a school belonging to a teacher called Francesc Galí. That school was also very different from the ones Joan had known before.

Guess what the schoolmaster, Mr. Galí, would have him do! He would blindfold him and have him feel an object —a water pitcher, a piece of fruit, a face— and then he would have him draw it. Have you ever tried to do that? It's a lot of fun! Besides having fun, he taught the young painter many other things that later helped him a lot.

Besides attending classes at Galí's school, his enthusiasm for doing things lead him to attend classes at the Llotja also where he was taught to paint in a totally different way and where he made friends who helped him to understand a lot of other things.

One fine day, in 1916, as he was strolling through the streets of Barcelona, he decided to go to visit an art gallery called Galeries Dalmau which he had heard about on account of the interesting things shown there.

He was surprised as he walked in because suddenly he discovered a new way to say things, a new way to understand painting.

Because the show had to do with French art, and new modern tendencies in particular, he began reading French poetry and French art magazines with great enthusiasm, and little by little he became overcome with a terrible urge to go to Paris.

For the time being, he fixed up a studio in his house and began painting things the same way he had seen them painted in that show that had impressed him so much, which consisted of taking forms and representing them by way of cubes or other geometric figures. (Two years later he managed to have his first one-man show in that very same gallery.)

Finally, one cold month of March, he picked up his belongings and left for Paris. He spent a rather gloomy winter there but when summer came he went back to Montroig; the countryside of that little town continued to be the fountain of inspiration for many of his paintings.

The next winter, the sculptor Pau Gargallo let him use his studio, but that young painter from Barcelona did not have such a good time there. Imagine how cold he must have been with the glass in the windows broken and the heater not working! And you know how cold it can get in Paris in winter!

Besides, he only had enough money to eat one hot meal a week, the rest of the time he had to eat dried figs that he had brought along from Montroig.

For a few years he continued to spend his summers in Montroig and his winters in Paris, where little by little he started selling his paintings. In spite of everything, his financial situation hadn't improved much.

One of the first paintings Miró sold was «La Masía» (The Farm), which like so many others, he began painting in Montroig. You see, in spite of the great appeal Paris held for him, the light, the open spaces and the Mediterranean air were most helpful for his inspiration.

OPERA COMIQUE
AVIAT
L'INSTANT
PARIS
MOET & CHANDON

Already in those difficult years, Joan dreamt of having a big, spacious studio where he could put all his paintings and his tools. Besides, the greater his desires to experiment, the greater his attraction for those materials that are not normally used in painting: wood, iron, cement and many others.

Years later, in 1956, his dream came true. He finally settled down in the studio that his good friend, the architect Josep-Lluis Sert, built for him on the island of Majorca. It was a great big studio with lots of light.

Ever since his early experiences in Francesc Galí's classes (Remember them?), Joan Miró kept discovering new ways to get to know objects. He had experimented how you can perceive things in a whole different, more enriching way with your hands.

Have you ever tried taking a piece of rope made out of different kinds of materials and checking —with your eyes closed and all your attention focused in the tips of your fingers— the different touches materials have? Some are rough to the touch, others are smooth.

Joan Miró did just that, and the result was a series of huge, gorgeous tapestries that are found in different parts of the world which he made with the help of a young tapestrymaker by the name of Josep Royo.

He was also curious about the touch of soils and of clay, and with his good friend Llorenç Artigas, he produced wonderful pieces of ceramics.

Joan Miró always said that he worked like a peasant. It was that great love he felt for his homeland that made him say «my strength comes from my feet» and what made him love the plain, simple things of life. Have you ever noticed how natural his works are? I'm sure you have. You won't see complicated lines and structures or strange colours. On the contrary, everything is clear and full of light —that light that he knew how to captivate from his homeland.

The forms that he draws are not all dressed up; they are few and simple. His colours are strong and bright, the colours you children like so much: blue, red, yellow, black, white. They are a song to happiness and to the imagination. They are works that readily touch the person's heart who knows how to look at them with humility and simplicity. That's right, the way you do.

Slowly on, that which Joan's father thought was nearly impossible and what seemed to him to be so hard to achieve, was becoming reality. His son was getting to be wellknown. Exhibitions of his work were being organized all over the world, from the United States —where he was asked to go from time to time— to Japan, France and many other countries. The name Joan Miró was beginning to carry a certain weight throughout the world. Museums were asking him for paintings and he was receiving important commissions from the highest institutions.

But don't think that all this was just luck or pure chance! Joan Miró always worked hard; he never stopped experimenting and so his work, after many years and a lot of hard work, ended up creating a clear, defined language of its own.

want it to be kept within the walls of a museum and so he did just that, he took it out into the street.

Joan Miró wanted to bequeath to his hometown the seeds of his work, sown all through the streets and squares and within everybody's reach. He didn't

So, when you are out strolling with your parents down the Rambla of Barcelona, take a look at the pavement and you will see a large mosaic with those familiar forms and colours. Or, when you go to play

at Escorxador Square, look up at that tall sculpture that seems to soar up to the sky, well, that also is one of Miró's works.

And if you go to the airport to say goodbye to a relative or a friend, take a good look at that big ceramic mural along the front of the building. Better yet, ask someone to take you to the Miró Foundation, the place where his art is alive and where you can walk around among the olive trees and the open spaces and see the work of that boy born in Barcelona.

Unfortunately, on Christmas Day, 1983, Joan Miró died. He died the same way he had lived, quietly. Yet, all the works of art he left us make it seem as if he were still alive, and the happy smiles on the faces of the children as they gaze at his work are a constant tribute to that great man, Joan Miró.